RAISING REPTILES

Divide Within 100

Mary Kaminski

ROSEN
COMMON CORE MATH
READERS

Rosen
Classroom™

New York

Published in 2015 by The Rosen Publishing Group, Inc.
29 East 21st Street, New York, NY 10010

Book Design: Jonathan J D'Rozario

Photo Credits: Cover Mila Semenova/Shutterstock.com; pp. 3, 4, 6, 8, 10, 12, 14, 16, 18, 20, 22, 23, 24 (background) ririro/
Shutterstock.com; pp. 3, 4, 6, 8, 10, 12, 14, 16, 18, 20, 22, 23, 24 (scale) Tatiana Yakovleva/Shutterstock.com; p. 5 My Good
Images/Shutterstock.com; p. 7 (icon) Michiel de Wit/Shutterstock.com; p. 7 (main) Charles Brutlag/Shutterstock.com;
pp. 7, 9, 11, 13, 15 (frame) garriphoto/Shutterstock.com; p. 9 (icon) taro911 Photographer/Shutterstock.com;
p. 9 (main) Nigel Pavitt/AWL Images/Getty Images; pp. 11, 15 Matt Jeppson/Shutterstock.com; p. 13 Anna Lurye/
Shutterstock.com; p. 17 Jay Ondreicka/Shutterstock.com; p. 19 Barcroft Media/Contributor/Getty Images; p. 21 Heiko Kiera/
Shutterstock.com; p. 22 itman_47/Shutterstock.com.

Library of Congress Cataloging-in-Publication Data
Kaminski, Mary, author.
Raising reptiles : divide within 100 / Mary Kaminski.
       pages cm. — (Math masters. Operations and algebraic thinking)
 Includes index.
ISBN 978-1-4777-4949-4 (pbk.)
ISBN 978-1-4777-4948-7 (6-pack)
ISBN 978-1-4777-6452-7 (library binding)
1. Division—Juvenile literature. 2. Arithmetic—Juvenile literature. 3. Reptiles—Juvenile literature. I. Title.
QA115.K36 2015
513.2′14—dc23
                                            2014004067
Manufactured in the United States of America

CPSIA Compliance Information: Batch #WS15RC: For further information contact Rosen Publishing, New York, New York at 1-800-237-9932.

Contents

At the Reptile House   4

Turtles and Tortoises   6

Lizards!   10

Slithering Snakes   16

American Alligator   20

Feeding the Animals   22

Glossary   23

Index   24

At the Reptile House

There are many kinds of animals in the world, but reptiles are my favorite! Reptiles have features that set them apart from other animals. They are covered with scales. Reptiles are cold-blooded, which means their body heat changes according to the heat of their **environment**. Some reptiles lay eggs, and some give birth to live babies.

I like to learn about reptiles firsthand. I **volunteer** at the reptile house at my local zoo! I help raise their reptiles.

Some reptiles, such as turtles and alligators, have scutes (SKOOTS) instead of scales. Scutes are hard, bony plates. This tortoise has a shell full of bony scutes!

Turtles and Tortoises

The first reptile I ever worked with was a turtle. I have a pet turtle at home, and it made me interested in learning more about reptiles.

There are many **species** of turtles, but they all have a shell. A turtle's shell is like a shield that keeps it safe from harm. Turtles can hide inside their shell when they see a predator coming. Turtles spend most of their life in water. Sea turtles almost never leave the water, but freshwater turtles climb out to rest in the sun.

Painted turtles can be red, green, black, and yellow. We have 12 painted turtles at the reptile house. They are in 2 cages with 6 turtles each. That means 12 divided by 2 is 6. You can check your answer by multiplying 2 times 6 to get 12.

$12 \div 2 = 6$

$6 \times 2 = 12$

Turtles and tortoises look a lot alike, but they're also very different! Tortoises spend their lives on land instead of in water. Tortoises like to live in hot, dry places instead of wet places. Also, tortoises have rounded feet for walking instead of flat feet for swimming.

We have African pancake tortoises in the reptile house. They're small tortoises that only grow to about 7 inches (18 cm) long. Unlike most tortoises, they run quickly!

African pancake tortoises eat grass and vegetables, but we give them melons for a treat. There are 18 melon pieces and 6 tortoises. Using division, I find out that each tortoise can have 3 pieces. I multiply 6 times 3 to make sure that's correct.

18 ÷ 6 = 3   6 x 3 = 18

Lizards!

We also have many lizards at the reptile house. There are about 5,000 species of lizards in the world! Many lizards spend their day lying in the sun. They need the sun to keep them warm because they're cold-blooded.

I take care of the geckos. Geckos are great climbers—some can even climb on walls! They have special hairs on their feet that help them stick to smooth surfaces. We have 21 geckos in 7 cages. There are 3 geckos in each cage.

To check my division, I multiply 7 times 3 to get 21. I can set up a triangle to show the connection between multiplication and division in an equation. The numbers 3, 7, and 21 are all connected!

21

x ÷

3   7

21 ÷ 7 = 3

7 x 3 = 21

One of the coolest lizards we have is the chameleon (kuh-MEEL-yuhn). There are many kinds of chameleons, but they all have big eyes and a curled tail. Most have a special ability—changing color! A chameleon can change color to blend in with its environment. Some chameleon colors are pink, blue, red, orange, and green.

These colorful critters are found in deserts and jungles in Africa and Asia. At the zoo, we feed our chameleons worms, berries, and insects.

> I have 27 worms to feed the chameleons. If I want to give 9 to each chameleon, I have enough to feed 3 chameleons. Can you set up a multiplication equation to check your answer? Use the triangle to help you find the answer!

27

x ÷

3   9

27 ÷ 9 = 3

9 x ? = 27

Geckos and chameleons are pretty small compared to the Gila (HEE-luh) monster! The Gila monster is the largest lizard in the United States. It can grow to over 2 feet (61 cm) long. This lizard has a **venomous** bite. This helps the lizard catch other animals for food.

Gila monsters are found in the deserts of the Southwest. They spend most of their lives underground and don't like to move around a lot.

Gila monsters like to eat eggs, bugs, and small animals. I feed the Gila monster 4 equal meals a day. If I feed it 32 bugs a day, how many bugs do I feed it each time? Check your answer using multiplication.

32

x ÷

?   4

32 ÷ 4 = ?

4 x ? = 32

Slithering Snakes

Some snakes can't harm people. Some people even keep them as pets. But some snakes are venomous, and that means they can be trouble!

Eastern diamondback rattlesnakes are venomous snakes found in the southeastern United States. They can grow up to 8 feet (2.4 m) long. Rattlesnakes are vipers, which means they have sharp teeth that put poison into their **prey** to kill it. They're called rattlesnakes because they have a rattle on their tail that they shake to warn predators to stay away.

We have an eastern diamondback rattlesnake at the zoo. We feed it 5 mice at a time. If we have 40 mice to feed the snake, how many meals will it have to eat? How can you check your answer?

$$40 \div 5 = ?$$

17

The longest snake we have at the zoo is the reticulated (rih-TIH-kyuh-lay-tuhd) python. This kind of python is the longest snake in the world and can grow up to 25 feet (7.6 m) long! They're found in Southeast Asia.

A reticulated python isn't venomous, but it's still a scary predator. A python hunts by catching its prey and then curling around the animal, squeezing until it dies. At the zoo, we feed it rats and rabbits.

If we have 42 rats to feed our python and I like to put 6 in its cage at a time, how many times can we feed the python?

$42 \div 6 = ?$

American Alligator

At the zoo, the longest four-legged reptile is the American alligator. It can grow to over 15 feet (4.6 m) long! It has tough skin made up of scutes.

Sometimes it's hard to tell the difference between an alligator and a crocodile. That's because alligators are part of the crocodile family. Both reptiles live in water and on land. But alligators like freshwater more than salt water, while crocodiles like salt water. Also, alligators have short, wide heads, while crocodiles have longer heads.

In the wild, female alligators lay about 35 to 90 eggs every summer. If a female alligator lays 66 eggs, how many groups of 11 eggs are there?

$$66 \div 11 = ?$$

Feeding the Animals

At the reptile house, I learn how to take care of many reptiles. I learn how to clean their cages and how warm each one has to be. I also learn what each animal eats and how to feed it.

I use division to help me feed the animals. Today, I get food ready for the Asian box turtles. If I have 81 pieces of lettuce and 9 turtles, how many pieces can I give each turtle?

Glossary

environment (ihn-VY-ruhn-muhnt) Everything that is around a living thing.

prey (PRAY) An animal that's hunted by other animals for food.

species (SPEE-sheez) A group of living things that are all the same kind.

venomous (VEH-nuh-muhs) Able to harm someone or something with a poison-filled bite or sting.

volunteer (vah-luhn-TIHR) To do something to help because you want to do it.

Index

alligators, 4, 20

chameleons, 12, 14

check your answer, 6, 10, 12, 14, 16

eggs, 4, 14, 20

geckos, 10, 14

Gila monster, 14

how many, 14, 16, 18, 20, 22

lizards, 10, 12, 14

multiply, 6, 8, 10, 12, 14

rattlesnakes, 16

reticulated python, 18

scales, 4

scutes, 4, 20

snakes, 16, 18

tortoises, 4, 8

triangle, 10, 12

turtles, 4, 6, 8, 22

Due to the changing nature of Internet links, The Rosen Publishing Group, Inc., has developed an online list of websites related to the subject of this book. This site is updated regularly. Please use this link to access the list: www.powerkidslinks.com/mm/oat/rrep